Language book

Jessie Reid
Margaret Donaldson

Contents

	Page		
Clues	2	Mr Slink the spy	28
Nutty and Batty	3	A mixed-up message	30
Nutty plays a trick	4	Are they the same?	32
What is it?	6	Favourite food	34
Surprise, surprise!	8	Descriptions	35
Special words for speaking	10	Postcard problems	36
Who went first?	12	Circus stories	37
The alphabet	14	Turn it round	38
Special names	16	More descriptions	40
Words about pictures	18	More games with words	41
The days of the week	20	All aboard the Ark	42
Emma's diary	21	Ally the elephant	43
Some ways to start a story	22	A new kind of adjective	44
Putting things in order	24	Double, double!	46
What kind of ball	26	Talking about animals	47

M
Macmillan Education

Clues

One day, Mandy and Jay went with Tim to hunt for treasure in an old castle. Tim had a spade to dig with, and Jay had a bag to carry the treasure.

They looked everywhere. Then Jay found a piece of paper with writing on it.

"Good!" said Tim. "Maybe it's a clue."

But some of the words were covered with mud. The children couldn't read them.

The paper looked like this.

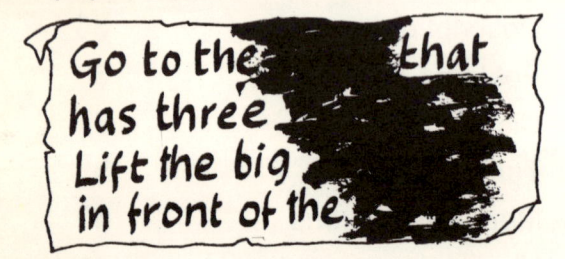

> Go to the ▓▓▓ that
> has three ▓▓▓
> Lift the big ▓▓▓
> in front of the ▓▓▓

Here are the missing words.

| windows | stones | fireplace | room |

Write

Write out the clue for the children. Put the missing words in the right places.

★ All the words you filled in are **names of things**.

Pretend you found an old box in a cellar. What was in it?
Begin like this: One day I went down into a cellar. It was dark and…

Nutty and Batty

Nutty and Batty live in a house with a red roof.

One day they decided to paint their house. So they went to a shop and they bought some paint and some brushes. They fetched a ladder from the shed, and put it against the wall. Batty said:

"Let's make the windows blue." So Nutty went up the ladder with some blue paint. Batty began to put yellow paint on the door. Soon Batty went to see what Nutty had done.

"You're stupid," he said to Nutty. "You've put paint all over the glass!"

Write

Find all the **names of things** in the story.
Write them in your own notebook.

When we write names one after the other, we say we are **making a list**.

Look at all the colours in the pictures on page 2 and page 3. Make a list of all the **colour names.** Can you add more colour names that you know?

Make a **list** of all the things you could use to make a model of a house.

Look at the picture, then finish this story about Nutty and Batty.

One day Batty told Nutty to saw a branch off a tree. Nutty went up the tree and began...

Nutty plays a trick

I'll put salt in the bowl instead of sugar! Batty will put it in his tea. Ha, ha!

Have some sugar.

1. Nutty and Batty liked to play tricks. One day Nutty emptied all the sugar out of the bowl and put salt into it **instead.**

2. Then Batty came in and made a cup of tea. He put a big spoonful of salt into his tea **instead of** sugar.

Ha, ha!

Ow! It tastes horrid.

Wait till I catch you!

3. Batty's tea tasted nasty. He was very angry when Nutty laughed at him.

4. He chased Nutty out of the house. Nutty was afraid, so he stayed outside for a long time **instead of** coming in.

Nutty emptied out the sugar and put in salt **instead.** He put salt **instead of** sugar.

Think of a trick for Batty to play on Nutty to get his own back. Write about it.

4

Here are some sentences. They are not about Nutty and Batty this time.

Write them out and fill in the spaces with one of these words.

puppy   water   honey

1. Sue had no milk so she drank some ___water___ instead.

2. Ian wanted a kitten but he got a ___puppy___ instead.

3. The jam is finished but you can have _____ instead.

We can say these another way.

4. Sue drank water instead of ___milk___ .

5. Ian got a puppy instead of a _____ .

6. You can have honey instead of _____ .

Now try these.

eating   wearing   saving

7. Pam spent her money instead of _____ it.

8. Pam kept her chocolate instead of _____ it.

9. Pam carried her coat instead of _____ it.

Now write them this way instead.

kept   carried   spent

10. Pam did not save her money. Instead, she _____ it.

11. Pam did not eat her chocolate. Instead, she _____ it.

12. Pam did not wear her coat. Instead, she _____ it.

What is it?

Ranjit and Mandy played a guessing game. Ranjit said:

"It eats grass and it gives you milk. Its name begins with **c** and has three letters."

Mandy said:

"That's easy. It's a cow."

Write

Here are more clues. Find the answers. The first five are names of animals.

1. It lives in Africa and it roars.
   Its name begins with **l** and has four letters.

2. You can ride on its back.
   Its name begins with **d** and has six letters.

3. It has no legs but it moves fast and can bite.
   Its name begins with **s** and has five letters.

4. It can live in the desert.
   Its name begins with **c** and has five letters.

5. It flies about at night. It has big eyes.
   Its name begins with **o** and has three letters.

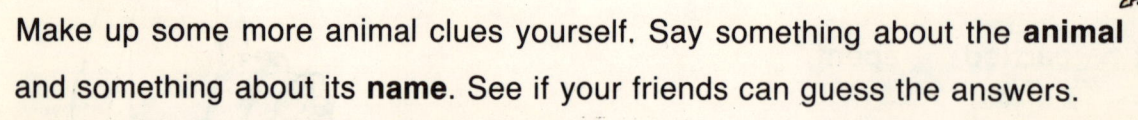

Make up some more animal clues yourself. Say something about the **animal** and something about its **name**. See if your friends can guess the answers. Begin by finishing this one.

It likes M_____ to drink. Its name begins with **c** and has _____ letters.

The next three are clues for things to play with.

1. It is round and it bounces.
   Its name begins with **b** and has four letters.

2. It is round but it doesn't bounce. It is often made of coloured glass. Its name begins with **m** and has six letters.

3. You can make it fly on a long string.
   Its name begins with **k** and has four letters.

Make up some clues for things you play with.

Say something about each **thing** and something about its **name.**

The next three are things to eat.

1. It is brown or white and it has a shell.
   Its name begins with **e** and has three letters.

2. It is brown or white and it has a crust.
   Its name begins with **b** and has five letters.

3. It grows in the ground. It has eyes and a skin.
   Its name begins with **p** and has six letters.

Now make up clues for these things in the same way.

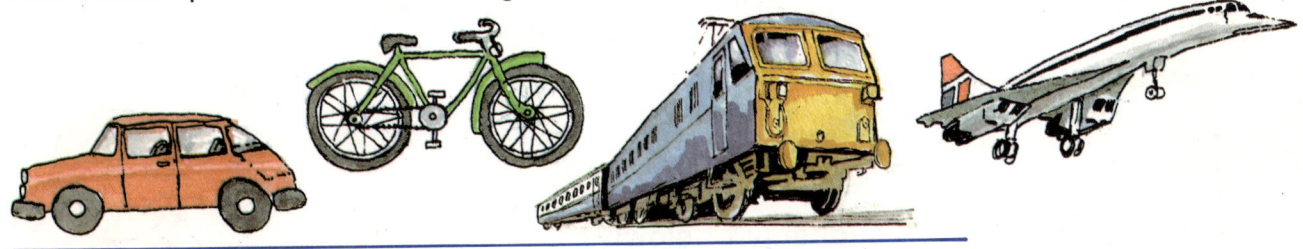

The words that are the answers to these clues are called **nouns.**

Nouns are name words.

7

Surprise, surprise!

Suddenly . . .

Aladdin rubbed his lamp.

Suddenly the genie appeared!

"What is your wish, master?" he asked.

Aladdin was very surprised.

★ When something happens **suddenly** that means you didn't expect it. It gives you a surprise.

Here are three ways to talk about a surprise.

| suddenly | all at once | all of a sudden |

Slowly . . .

Hansel and Gretel were alone in the forest.

Slowly it began to get dark. They knew it would soon be night-time and they were afraid.

Here are three ways to talk about things that happen **slowly**.

| slowly | gradually | little by little |

Write

Do these things happen **suddenly** or **slowly**?

1. a balloon bursting
2. a flower growing
3. a telephone ringing
4. a puddle drying up

Write

Use the words in the boxes on page 8 to fill the spaces in these sentences. Use different words each time.

1. The cat came creeping through the long grass.

    _____ it came nearer to the little bird.

2. _____ Jack ran into the room, shouting "Help!"

3. _____ the shadows grew longer and longer.

4. Jane left her ice cream on the table.

    _____ it melted.

5. Red Riding Hood was walking through the forest. _____ she met a wolf.

6. Miss Muffet was eating her curds and whey. _____ a great spider came along.

Pretend you found a wonderful lamp like Aladdin's. What happened when you rubbed it? Begin like this:

One day I found an old lamp in a heap of rubbish. I tried to clean it with my handkerchief. All at once...

Fascinating fact

Do you know what a **glacier** is? It is a river of ice. It moves gradually downhill. It may move only one or two metres in a year.

Special words for speaking

★ What can you use instead of **said**? Read this story.

Old Mrs Brown is deaf. She can't hear what people say. One day old Mrs Brown met Mrs Jones.

"It's cold today," said Mrs Jones.

"What did you say?" asked old Mrs Brown.

Mrs Jones made her voice louder.

"It's cold today," she shouted.

"What did you say?" asked old Mrs Brown again.

Mrs Jones made her voice louder still.

"IT'S COLD TODAY," she yelled.

"Don't shout at me," replied old Mrs Brown, crossly. "Everybody will think I am deaf."

★ The story does not use **said** every time that somebody speaks.

It uses **asked** when Mrs Brown asks a question.

It uses **replied** when Mrs Brown answers Mrs Jones.

It tells us how Mrs Brown speaks. It uses **shouted** and **yelled** when she speaks very loudly.

Fascinating fact

In St Paul's Cathedral in London there is a place called the Whispering Gallery. It is high up near the dome. If you speak in a whisper people can easily hear you on the other side of the gallery.

Write

Read this story and choose the best words for the spaces. Write the numbers and the words in your book.

| said | replied | asked | shouted | yelled |

One day Nutty fell into a hole in the road.

"Help!" he ___(1)___ . Nobody came.

He made his voice louder. "HELP!" he ___(2)___ .

Batty came along. He looked into the hole and saw Nutty.

"What are you doing down there?" he ___(3)___ .

"I fell in," ___(4)___ Nutty. "Help me to get out."

So Batty jumped into the hole as well.

"You are stupid!" ___(5)___ Nutty. "Now we are both in the hole."

Can you write the next bit of the story? How did Nutty and Batty get out of the hole? Make your story funny. Draw a picture for it.

1. Don't tell anyone.
2. Help!
3. Oh! my head!

How are the people in these pictures speaking? Choose the best word.

| screaming | groaning | whispering |

Can you think of more special words for speaking? Make a list of them.

11

Who went first?

One day Mandy and Jay went to play on the slide. Mandy went down the slide first. Jay went second.
Then Jay said:
"It's my turn to go first now."
So Jay went first and Mandy went second.

⭐ The first time, the children went in one **order.**
The next time, they went in another **order.**
Mandy first, Jay second is one order.
Jay first, Mandy second is another order.

The next day Tim came to play on the slide with Jay. Mandy was not there.

✏️ Write the two orders that Tim and Jay could go in.
Use the words **first** and **second**.
Make pictures for the two orders.

The next day Tim and Jay and Mandy were all playing on the slide.
The pictures show you how they went down.

✏️ Write the order for each picture in your book, like this:

___Jay___ first, _____ second, _____ third.

12

Now write the **orders** for these pictures.

This time just put the **names** in the right order.

You don't need to write **first, second** and **third**.

Can you think of any more orders they could go in?

Write them down. Just write the names.

Look at these words: **up go**

Here are the same words
in another order: **go up**

Write these words in another order.

1. table the
2. gone all
3. burns fire
4. me help
5. moon yellow
6. birthday happy
7. sweets some
8. away run
9. teacher my

What difference does it make when you put them in the other order?

Puzzle corner

Chris has a blue shirt. Ian has fair hair. Len has a red shirt.

Ann has black hair. Eric has a badge.

Write their names in the same order as the pictures.

The first letters will spell the name of a girl. Write her name.

13

The alphabet

We write words with letters.
We can write thousands of words, but
we do it with just twenty-six letters.

Here they are:

a b c d e f g h i j k l m n o p q r s t u v w x y z

axe run play hill swim zoo queen dig very elephant jump black fairy

These words use all the letters of the alphabet.

★ These letters are called the **alphabet**.
The way they are written here is called **alphabetical order**.

Ask your teacher to show you the class register.
It has your surnames in **alphabetical order**.
Can you think why?
Find your name in the register.

Here is a rhyme to help you to learn the alphabet.

a b c d e	A house up in a tree
e f g h i	A kite up in the sky
i j k l m	Three flowers upon a stem
m n o p q	A lion in the zoo
q r s t u	A yellow kangaroo
u v w x y	Two big fish to fry
y z-z-z-z	Time to go to bed!

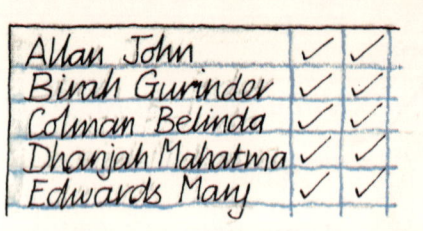

★ The alphabet at the top of this page is written in **small** letters.
Printers call them **lower case letters.**
Here is the alphabet in **capital** letters.
Printers call them **upper case letters**.

A B C D E F G H I J K L M N O P Q R S T U V W X Y Z

a b c d e f g h i j k l m n o p q r s t u v w x y z

Find the letter that comes **first** in alphabetical order:

1. **m** or **n**?
2. **h** or **g**?
3. **r** or **s**?
4. **k** or **j**?
5. **m** or **l**?
6. **v** or **u**?
7. **d** or **c**?
8. **p** or **q**?
9. **z** or **y**?

This time the letters are not all beside each other in the alphabet. Which comes first?

1. **b** or **d**?
2. **g** or **e**?
3. **o** or **m**?
4. **p** or **t**?
5. **m** or **h**?
6. **i** or **n**?
7. **f** or **j**?
8. **l** or **k**?
9. **t** or **w**?

Sometimes notices are written in capital letters, like this:

FOOD   STOP

Where would you see these notices?

Here are four more words that you can find on notices.

| telephone | danger | private | exit |

Write each one in capital letters. Then say where you might see it, and what it tells you.

Make a food alphabet. Try to find a food word for each letter of the alphabet. You could begin: **A**pple, **b**read, . . .
See if your friends have chosen the same words as you have.

15

Special names

The girls are eating cake. The dogs are watching them. They want some cake too.

The girls are called Beth and Mary.

Beth and **Mary** are their **special names.**

The dogs' **special names** are **Woof** and **Ginger**.

The other things in the picture don't have special names.

They are just called **a table,** or **a chair,** or **a plate.**

⭐ People always have **special names.**

Things sometimes have **special names,** like this ship.

✏️ Can you think of some more things that have special names?

Make a list of them. Begin each one with a capital letter.

Towns and countries have special names too. So do streets and schools.

⭐ **Special name** words are called **proper nouns.**

They always begin with a capital letter.

The words of your own name are **proper nouns.**

Write your name. Write the names of the people in your family.

Now finish these sentences.

1. I live in a place called _____ .
2. I live in a street called _____ .
3. My school is called _____ .
4. My friend is called _____ .
5. My teacher is called _____ .

16

Here are some special names
of places.

> **London   France**
> **Everest   The Atlantic**

Here are the names of
the **kind of place** each one is.

> **a mountain   an ocean**
> **a city   a country**

Match them up. Write a sentence about each place.

Begin: *London is...*

Here are some of the animals in the book called
Winnie-the-Pooh, with their special names.

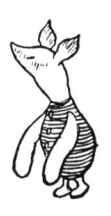

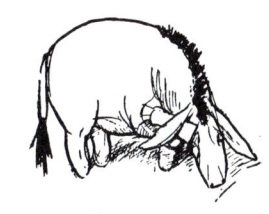

Winnie-the-Pooh   Kanga   Piglet   Eeyore

Here are the names of the **kind of animal** each one is.

> **a little pig   a donkey   a bear   a kangaroo**

Match them up. Write a sentence about each one.

Begin: *Piglet is...*

Do you have a pet at home or in school?

What **kind of animal** is it? What is its special name?

Write about it. Begin:

We have a pet...

17

Words about pictures

Here is a picture of Coco. Coco is a clown.

The words under the picture tell you

his special name and the kind of person he is.

Draw Coco and write the words under your picture.

Coco the clown.

Here is a picture of Jenny.

Jenny is a policewoman.

Read the words under the picture.

Draw Jenny and write the words under your picture.

Jenny the policewoman

Draw these pictures and write the words to go under them.

Here is Jack.
He is a sailor.

1. Jack the _____ .

Here is Debbie.
She is a doctor.

2. Debbie the _____ .

Here is Wanda.
She is a witch.

3. ____ ___ _____ .

Here is Hugo.
He is a dragon.

4. ____ ___ _____ .

Here is Dinah.
She is a dolphin.

5. ____ ___ _____ .

Here is Len.
He is a postman.

6. ____ ___ _____ .

18

The words under the pictures can go into sentences.

Put the right words in each sentence.

Make sentences like this one:

> I saw Jenny the policewoman catching a thief.

1. I saw Coco ___ _____ in the circus.

2. I saw _____ ___ _____ in his cave.

3. _____ ___ _____ was on his ship.

4. _____ ___ _____ was swimming in her pool.

5. I saw ___ ___ _____ with some letters.

6. _____ ___ _____ worked in a hospital.

7. I saw _____ ___ _____ on her broomstick.

Make up a poem about Wanda the Witch.

Here is one way you could begin.

Wanda the witch lives in the deep dark wood...

You can begin in a different way if you like.

Read your poem to your friends.

Have you read about Mrs Wobble the Waitress? There is a story about her by Allan and Janet Ahlberg.

Make up some more names like hers for a **diver**, a **firefighter**, a **gardener** and a **nurse.** Can you think of any more?

19

The days of the week

Here are the special names of the days of the week.

They always come in this order.

Sunday   Monday   Tuesday   Wednesday

Thursday   Friday   Saturday

Then it's Sunday again!

Saturday and Sunday are called the **weekend.**

⭐ You can see the days of the week written in a **calendar.**

Can you think of some other places where you can see them?

1. Which day comes after Wednesday?
2. Which day comes before Sunday?
3. Which day comes between Monday and Wednesday?
4. Which day comes between Saturday and Monday?
5. Find out which day of the week it is **today**.
6. Which day was **yesterday**?
7. Which day will **tomorrow** be?
8. Which day has the longest name?

   How many letters does its name have?

20

Emma's diary

Emma keeps a diary.

She writes something about every day.

She writes about Saturday and Sunday too.

Here is a page from Emma's diary.

Monday	We had painting in school. I painted a volcano.
Tuesday	We had fire drill today.
Wednesday	Today is my birthday. I am eight. I got a watch from my mum.
Thursday	I started a new story book today.
Friday	I fell in the playground today and hurt my knee.
Saturday	I had my birthday tea with my friends.
Sunday	I went to see my Grannie. She gave me some chocolate.

Which do you think was Emma's best day? Why do you think so?

Make a page of your book into a diary for one week, like Emma's.

Every day, write about something that happened or something you did. Which day was the best?

Fascinating fact

The captain of a ship has to keep a diary.

It is called the ship's **log**.

The log that was kept by Captain Cook tells how he discovered Australia and New Zealand.

Some ways to start a story

How do stories start?

They can start in lots of ways, but here are some you will find in your books.

Long ago stories

The story of Cinderella could begin:

Once upon a time there was a girl called Cinderella . . .

Or it could begin:

There was once a girl called Cinderella . . .

The story of the Three Bears could begin:

Once upon a time there were Three Bears . . .

Or it could begin:

There were once Three Bears . . .

Here is another way to start:

A very long time ago, a King lived in a great palace.

⭐ Stories have names. The name of a story is called its **title**.

If you have a book of stories, the **titles** are all in a list at the beginning.

This list is called the **contents**. The list gives you the page where each story begins. It helps you to find a story you want to read.

Find a book of stories in your class library.

Look at the titles. Look at the ways the stories begin.

Do they make you want to read the rest of the story?

Talk about them with your teacher or your friends.

Here are three pictures. Each one is for a different story.

(1)

(2)

(3)

Here are three story **titles.** Each one goes with one of the pictures.

| The girl who could fly | How the monkey got his long tail | The princess who would not eat |

Here are the beginnings of the three stories.

Once there lived a king and queen who had a beautiful daughter.

Clare was a girl who loved birds.

When monkeys first came to live in the forest, they did not have long tails.

Write the number (1) for the first picture in your notebook.

Then write the **title** and the **story beginning** that go with it.

Do the same for the other pictures.

Choose one of the stories and finish it in your own way.

Putting things in order

a b c d e f g h i j k l m n o p q r s t u v w x y z
A B C D E F G H I J K L M N O P Q R S T U V W X Y Z

Here are the names of some people in stories and rhymes.

Write them in **alphabetical order.** Look at the first letter each time.

| Jack   Aladdin   Cinderella   Rumpelstiltskin   Gretel |

Make a list of six things you can see in your classroom.

Choose words that begin with different letters.

Write the words in **alphabetical order**.

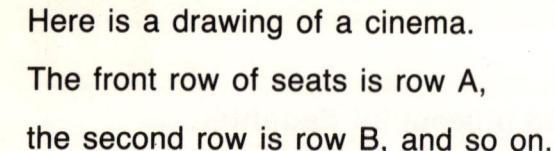

Here is a drawing of a cinema.

The front row of seats is row A,

the second row is row B, and so on.

Four families are at the cinema.

The Ross family is in Row C.

The Brown family is in Row B.

The Trent family is in Row F.

The Briggs family is in Row D.

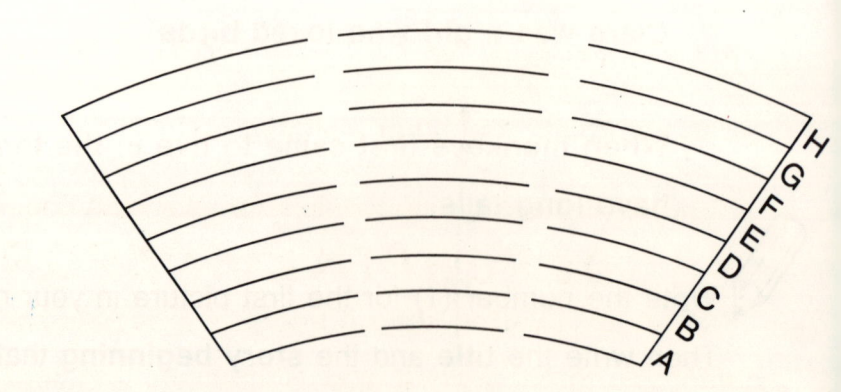

Draw the cinema and put in the names of the families to show where they are sitting.

24

1. Which family is just behind the Browns?
2. How many families are in front of the Trents?
3. How many families are behind the Rosses?
4. Which rows are empty?

Secret writing

You can do secret writing with the alphabet. Here is one way.

Suppose you want to write **help.**

Take each letter in the word and look for the letter that comes **after** it in the alphabet. Write that letter instead.

h   The letter after **h** is **i**, so instead of **h** write **i**
e   The letter after **e** is **f**, so instead of **e** write **f**
l   The letter after **l** is **m**, so instead of **l** write **m**
p   The letter after **p** is **q**, so instead of **p** write **q**

So instead of *help* you write *ifmq*

Write your name in the secret writing.

Write your friend's name in the secret writing.

★ This kind of secret writing is called a **code.**

Put this message into the code: *I have found the treasure.*

Can you think of another alphabet code?

Make up a message and write it in your own code.

A B C D E F G H I J K L M N O P Q R S T U V W X Y Z

If a girl asks you to **keep a secret** she means she doesn't want you to tell anyone else. Sometimes it is hard to keep a secret. Write a story about a girl or a boy who kept a secret for a friend when it was not easy.

25

What kind of ball?

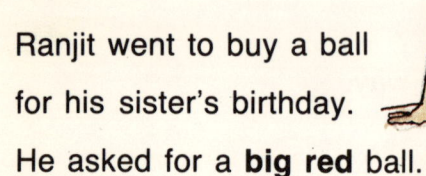

Ranjit went to buy a ball for his sister's birthday. He asked for a **big red** ball.

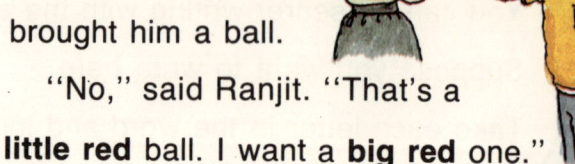

The girl in the shop brought him a ball.
"No," said Ranjit. "That's a **little red** ball. I want a **big red** one."

The girl brought another ball.
"No," said Ranjit. "That's a **big blue** ball. I want a **big red** one."

The girl brought another ball.
"Good," said Ranjit. "That's a **big red** ball. It's lovely".

★ The words **big** and **red** tell us about the ball that Ranjit wanted.
We say they **describe** the ball. They are called **adjectives.**
We use adjectives to **describe** things.

Put the right adjective in each space.

1. Ranjit did not want a little ball. He wanted a _____ one.

   But the girl did not bring a _____ one.

   Instead, she brought a _____ one.

26

2. Ranjit wanted a _____ ball, not a blue one.

   But the girl brought a _____ one instead of a

   _____ one.

3. At last, the girl brought a ____ ____ ball.

   Ranjit said it was _____ .

How many different adjectives did you put in the sentences? Write them out.

Here are four girls.

Ann **Sue** **Pat** **Jacky**

Here are four adjectives to tell us about their hair.

| long | short | straight | curly |

Look at the pictures and put in **two** adjectives for each girl.

1. Ann has ____ ____ hair.   2. Pat has ____ ____ hair.

3. Sue has ____ ____ hair.   4. Jacky has ____ ____ hair.

Fascinating fact

Adjectives are often used for **surnames**.

People can be called **Black,** or **Green,** or **Long,** or **Short,** or **Thin,** or **Stout.** Can you think of some more?

⭐ When the words are used for surnames, they are not adjectives any more.

They are **proper nouns.**

27

Mr Slink the spy

Mr Slink is a spy. He tries to steal secret papers, so he does not want anyone to know who he is. Sometimes he wears dark glasses.
Sometimes he wears a black beard.
Sometimes he wears a white beard.
Sometimes he wears a moustache.

1. On Monday, Mr Slink wore dark glasses **only**.
   He didn't wear a beard or a moustache.

2. On Tuesday, Mr Slink wore a white beard **instead of** dark glasses.
   Draw Mr Slink the way he looked on Tuesday.

3. On Wednesday, Mr Slink wore dark glasses and a white beard **as well.**
   Read the writing under the picture.

4. On Thursday, Mr Slink wore a black beard **only**.
   Draw him the way he looked on Thursday.
   Write under your picture to say what it is.

5. On Friday, Mr Slink wore a moustache **as well as** a black beard.
   Read the writing under the picture.

6. On Saturday, Mr Slink wore a moustache **only**.
   Draw him the way he looked on Saturday.
   Write under your picture.

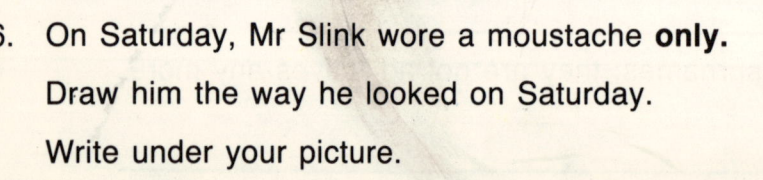

Mr Slink wearing dark glasses only.

Mr Slink wearing dark glasses and a white beard as well.

Mr Slink with a moustache as well as a black beard.

Find the right day for each space, and write the sentences.

1. On _____ he wore a white beard only.
2. On _____ he wore a black beard only.
3. On _____ he wore a black beard and a moustache as well.
4. On _____ he wore a moustache but not a beard.

⭐ When Mr Slink puts on a beard or a moustache we say he is wearing a **disguise.** He puts them on to **disguise** himself.

Make up a story. Begin like this:

> One day Mr Slink the spy was in a cafe. He was wearing a moustache and dark glasses to disguise himself. He ordered some coffee. Suddenly his moustache fell off...

Puzzle corner

Here is a word written in the secret **code** on page 25. `dpnf`
To find out what it means, you have to go **back** one letter in the alphabet every time. Then you get `come`
Here is a secret message. What does it mean?

Dpnf up nz ipvtf bgufs tdippm

A mixed-up message

Nutty sent Batty a funny message. Batty read it.

It said: "Like I babies jelly." Batty said: "That's nonsense."

Nutty said: "I know it is. The words are in the wrong order. You have to put them in the right order."

Batty said: "I like babies jelly." "Wrong!" Nutty said. "Try again."

"I know!" said Batty. "I like jelly babies." And that was the answer.

Here are more mixed-up messages. Put the words in the right order so that they make sense.

1. and play come
2. we late are
3. that me give
4. to bed go
5. it raining is
6. cat the sleeping is
7. him at look
8. is pencil broken my
9. like I ice-cream
10. not I tired am

This time, the mixed-up words are all from nursery rhymes. Begin with the word that has a capital letter.

1. wall on a Humpty-Dumpty sat
2. mouse The ran clock the up
3. sixpence song of a Sing
4. black sheep any have wool you Ba-Ba?
5. down and crown broke his Jack fell
6. old an There woman was

Make up a message for one of your friends. Then write it with the words in the wrong order. See if your friend can put them in the right order.

Puzzle corner

Try this crossword. The numbers show where the words begin.

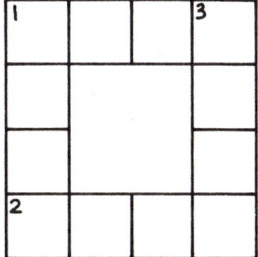

Across

1. You wear it in cold weather.
2. You carry plates on it.

Down

1. A horse can pull it.
3. Very small.

Fascinating fact

If you have 3 words, you can put them in 6 different orders. (Look back at page 13. The three children can go down the slide in six different orders.)

If you have 4 words, you can put them in 24 different orders.

If you have 5 words, you can put them in 120 different orders!

But most of these wouldn't make sense!

Are they the same?

The big dog has a big bone. The little dog has a big bone **too**.

The fat lady has two dogs. The thin lady has **only** one dog.

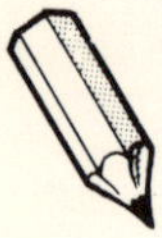

Now finish these. Fill in three words each time.

Think whether you have to use **too** or **only**.

1. The big boy has a balloon.

   The little boy has __ ____ ____ .

2. The car has four wheels.

   The bike has ____ ____ ____ .

3. The blue boat has one sail.

   The red boat has __ ____ ____ .

4. The big house has three windows.

   The little house has ____ ____ ____ .

5. A dog has four legs.

   A boy has ____ ____ ____ .

6. A bird has a tail.

   A rabbit has __ ____ ____ .

The big dog hasn't got a bone. Nutty doesn't like cold weather.

The little dog hasn't got **one either**. Batty doesn't like **it either**.

Finish these little stories. Use the words in one of the boxes each time.

| it either | one either |

1. The little clown can't reach the shelf.

   The big clown can't reach ___ ___ .

2. The big girl hasn't got a cake.

   The little girl hasn't got ___ ___ .

3. The cat doesn't like the dog.

   The postman doesn't like ___ ___ .

4. Nutty can't drive a car.

   Batty can't drive ___ ___ .

Tell this story in your own words.

33

Favourite food

Here are three bears, with the things they like to eat.
These sentences tell you what the bears like to eat.
Put one word in each space so as to make sense.

| only | too | instead | either |

1. Grumpy the big bear likes porridge _____.

   He doesn't like nuts. He doesn't like honey _____.

2. Humpy the middle-sized bear likes nuts best.

   But she likes porridge _____.

3. Dumpy the little bear doesn't eat nuts

   and he doesn't eat porridge _____.

   _____, he eats honey.

If you like some food better than anything else, you can say it is your **favourite** food.

1. Grumpy's favourite food is _____ .
2. Humpy's favourite food is _____ .
3. Dumpy's favourite food is _____ .

Imagine that a magician brings you
all your favourite things to eat.

Begin: *One day I was sitting at home.*
I was thinking of lovely things to eat.
I wished...

34

Descriptions

Tim wrote a description of one of his friends.

He wrote:

*My friend is fairly tall and quite fat.
She has black curly hair and dark brown eyes.
Her teeth are very white and shiny.
She is energetic and cheerful, but sometimes she is rather cheeky.*

Tim asked Mandy to guess who it was.

Mandy read Tim's description and said: "I know! It's Jay!"

⭐ Tim said Jay was **fairly tall.** That means Jay is not small, but not very tall either. He said Jay was **quite fat.** That means Jay is not thin, but not very fat either. He said she was **rather cheeky.** What do you think that means?

✏️ Describe one of your friends the way Tim did.
You can use some words from the boxes.

| fairly | very | quite | rather |

Is your friend tall or small, fat or thin?
Write about your friend's **hair** and **eyes.**
Write about the kind of person your friend is.

| shy | quiet | cheerful | noisy | clever |
| cheeky | helpful |

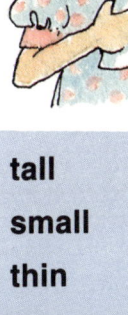

tall
small
thin
fat
plump

long
short
curly
straight

dark
fair
blue
brown
red
hazel

35

Postcard problems

Nutty went for a holiday to the seaside.

He sent Batty a postcard. But the dog found it

and tore it up!

Batty tried to fit the pieces together again.

This is how it looked.

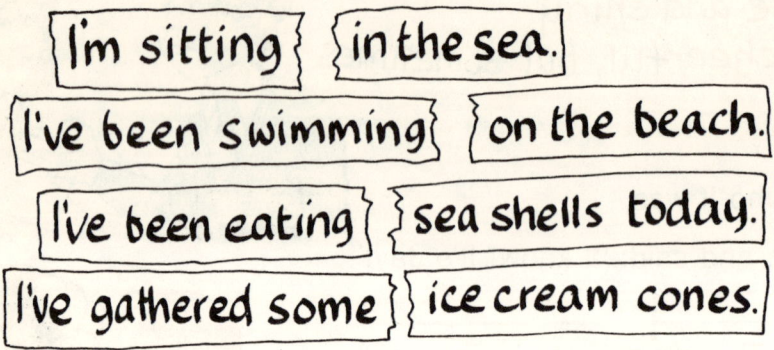

I'm sitting	in the sea.
I've been swimming	on the beach.
I've been eating	sea shells today.
I've gathered some	ice cream cones.

"Oh dear," said Batty. "What a funny holiday!"

Put the right pieces together. Write out Nutty's postcard.

Nutty sent another postcard, and the dog tore it up again!
When Batty tried to put the pieces together,

this is how it looked.

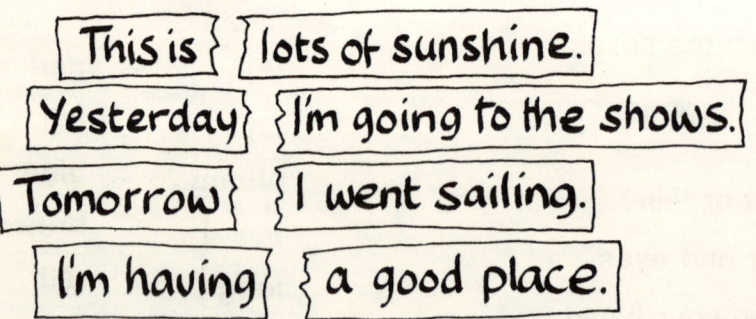

This is	lots of sunshine.
Yesterday	I'm going to the shows.
Tomorrow	I went sailing.
I'm having	a good place.

Put the right pieces together, and write out Nutty's postcard.

Make up another puzzle like these. See if your friend

can fit the torn-up pieces together.

Circus stories

Look at these pictures. They show you something that happened in the circus.

Here are three sentences to tell the story. Put them in the **right order.**

Suddenly his ladder fell over.

The paint pot fell on the big clown.

One day the little clown was painting.

Here is another story in pictures.

Here are the beginnings of three sentences to tell the story.
Use them in the **right order** and finish each one yourself.

Suddenly the big clown . . .

One day the little clown . . .

The little clown . . .

Make up another circus story.

Draw three pictures to show what happened.

Write a sentence about each picture.

Turn it round

Look at the sentence underneath the pictures.

Cheeky the chimp hid in a box, then he jumped out.

Look at the sentence again. We can write it in another order instead. We can write:

Cheeky the chimp hid in a box, then **out** he jumped.

The word **out** is in a different place now.

Change these sentences round in the same way.

1. Cheeky the chimp found a hat and he ran **off** with it.

   Cheeky the chimp found a hat and **off**.................

2. The little clown pushed the ladder and it fell **down** with a crash.

   The little clown pushed the ladder and **down**...................

Now look at the next sentences.

3. The acrobat took hold of the rope, then he climbed **up.**

4. The chimp found his bicycle and he rode **away** on it.

Draw the pictures for 3. and 4.

Change the sentences round and write them underneath the pictures.

38

Jack slipped and fell. He tumbled down the hill.

Instead of writing: "He tumbled **down the hill**"
we can put the words in a different order.
We can start with **"Down the hill"**.

He tumbled **down the hill.**

So we get: "**Down the hill** he tumbled."
Look at this new sentence. You will see that the word **Down** starts with a capital letter now and the word **he** starts with a small letter.

Change these sentences round in the same way.

1. Jane stood still. She saw two eyes in the darkness.

   Jane stood still. In ....

2. Robert listened. He could hear a noise in the distance.

   Robert listened. In ....

3. Tim awoke. He saw a little man at the foot of the bed.

   Tim awoke. At ....

Now do these.

This time you can turn **both** sentences round the other way.

4. Mary likes cornflakes for breakfast. She likes toast and cheese for supper.

   For ....   For ....

5. Swallows fly away in autumn. They come back in spring.
6. The sun sets at night. It rises in the morning.

More descriptions

Here is a picture of Tim in fancy dress.
He is wearing a pirate's costume.
Finish these sentences to **describe** him.

    On his head he has . . .

    On his feet he has . . .

    Round his waist he . . .

    In his hand he . . .

    On his shoulder . . .

Draw yourself in fancy dress.

Describe your costume in the same way.

The land of story-books

    At evening when the lamp is lit,

    Around the fire my parents sit;

    They sit at home and talk and sing,

    And do not play at anything.

    Now, with my little gun I crawl

    All in the dark along the wall,

    And follow round the forest track

    Away behind the sofa back.

    There, in the night, where none can spy,

    All in the hunter's camp I lie,

    And play at books that I have read

    Till it is time to go to bed. *(Robert Louis Stevenson)*

What games do you play at home? Write about some of them.

More games with words

You can make a list of words from these letters.

sadhiylo

See how many you can make. You may use any letter twice, or three times, in one word. Here are two words to start you off.

    dad   **lay**

Can you make a word which uses all the letters? If you are allowed to use the letter **e** as well, how many extra words can you make?

If you put the letters in the word **step** in the opposite order you make the word **pets.**
Turn these words round in the same way and write them in your notebook.
Draw a line under the ones that make new words.

was	wasp	pots	reed	rain	on	in
rat	part	rats	lid	red	mum	dad

⭐ The words **mum** and **dad** are not like the others. What's different about them?

Here are some mixed-up questions. Put the words in the right order and then answer each question. Remember to put in the capital letters.

1. you old how are?
2. legs a how dog many has?
3. has animal trunk a which?
4. are teeth your where?

All aboard the Ark

Do you know the story of Noah's Ark?

Noah built a huge boat because a flood was coming.

He called his boat the Ark. He took two animals of each kind into it to save them from being drowned.

They all went in two by two.

Here are the **names** of some of them.

snakes	horses	frogs
mice	doves	tigers

Here are words for **how they moved.**

scurried	slithered	bounded
flew	hopped	galloped

Choose the best word for the way each animal moved.

Put them in sentences, like this:

The snakes _____ into the Ark.

How do you think the animals **ate their food**?

Choose the best word for each animal.

Put each word in a sentence.

nibbled	gulped	gnawed
munched	snapped	pecked

What **sounds** do you think the animals made?

Make up your own sentences this time.

42

Ally the elephant

In this story, some of the words have been left out.
They are in this box. Find the right word for each space.

eat	come	went	told
shut	let	saw	

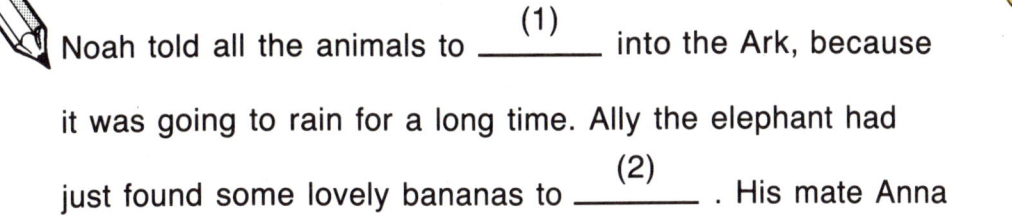

Noah told all the animals to _____(1)_____ into the Ark, because it was going to rain for a long time. Ally the elephant had just found some lovely bananas to _____(2)_____ . His mate Anna _____(3)_____ him to hurry, but Ally wanted to finish his dinner. So she _____(4)_____ on by herself.

Suddenly Ally _____(5)_____ that the water was up to his knees! He started to run to the Ark. Noah was just going to _____(6)_____ the door! "Wait for me!" Ally trumpeted, and Noah _____(7)_____ him in just in time.

★ All the words you filled in are words for **what people or animals did.** These words have a special name. They are called **verbs.**

Look at the words on page 42 that tell how the animals **moved.** These are **verbs** also. Make a list of more **moving verbs.**

Look at the words for how the animals **ate.** These are **verbs** also. Make a list of more **eating verbs.**

43

A new kind of adjective

Here is a picture of Sally. Sally has long hair.

We can write: Sally is **long-haired.**

If you write it this way you have to put the letters **ed** on the end of the word **hair.**

And you have to put a little line between **long** and **haired.**

This little line is called a **hyphen.**

When you put a hyphen between **long** and **haired** you make a new kind of **adjective.**

Draw a **short-haired** girl. Write the words: **a short-haired girl** under your picture. Remember to put in the hyphen.

Write these sentences and fill in the spaces. Remember to put in the hyphen every time.

1. The dog has a short tail. It is a _____ dog.

2. The boy has curly hair. He is a _____ boy.

3. The house has a red roof. It is a _____ house.

4. The garden has a high wall. It is a _____ garden.

Here is a picture of a puppy. It has a white tail and a black nose. It is **white-tailed** and **black-nosed.**

⭐ You will see that you have to put the letters **ed** on the end of tail, but you have to put **d** only on the end of **nose.** This is because **nose** has **e** on the end of it already.

✏️ Now write these sentences and fill in the spaces.

1. The man has a loud voice. He is a _____ man.

2. The woman has a red face. She is a _____ woman.

Draw Rudolph the red-nosed reindeer. Write under your picture to say what it is.

This hand has long fingers. It is **long-fingered.**

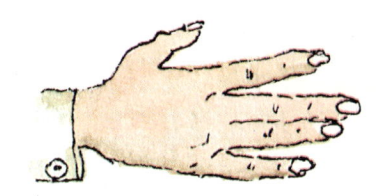

⭐ Look at the words **fingers** and **fingered.** You will see that you have to take off the letter **s** before you put on the letters **ed.**

✏️ Draw a monster with green eyes. Write **a green-eyed monster** under your picture. Don't forget the hyphen.

Write these sentences and fill in the spaces. Use an adjective like **green-eyed** or **long-fingered** for each one.

1. The boat has tall masts. It is _____ .

2. The coat has many colours. It is _____ .

3. The house has four rooms. It is _____ .

4. The dragon has two tails. It is _____ .

Draw a dragon with three tails. Write under your picture to say what it is. Write a story about it.

45

Double, double!

This fly has long legs. So we can say it is a **long-legged** fly.

★ When we write **long-legged** we have to put two **g**'s.
We double the last letter of **leg** and add on **ed**.
When we put the same letter twice instead of just once we **double** it.

✏ Now make some adjectives to fill in these spaces.

Remember to **double** the letter before you add **ed**.

1. This flower has a short stem.

    It is a _____ flower.

2. This apple has a green skin.

    It is a _____ apple.

3. That mountain has a white top.

    It is a _____ mountain.

4. This beetle has red spots.

    It is a _____ beetle.

✏ Draw   a long-tailed dinosaur   a black-faced sheep

          a red-skinned apple   a three-wheeled car

Write the correct words under each picture.

★ You have just written a **caption** under each picture. **Captions** are words that we put **under pictures**. They **tell about** the picture.

46

Talking about animals

This Siamese cat has blue eyes.

But many cats don't have blue eyes.

Their eyes may be green or golden.

The Siamese cat in the picture has four legs.

All cats have four legs (if they haven't had an accident!).

So we can write: **Cats have four legs.**

Or we can write: **Cats are four-legged animals.**

Here are some more sentences about animals.

Some of them are about things that **all** animals have.

Others are about things that **some** animals have.

Write the sentences out and choose words to fill the spaces.

| fur | blue eyes | wool | stripes |
| spots | fins | feathers | |

1. All ostriches have _____ .
2. All sheep have _____ .
3. Some dogs have _____ .
4. All fish have _____ .
5. Some fish have _____ .
6. All cats have _____ .
7. Some cats have _____ .

47

All tigers eat meat.

★ We can say this another way.

We can say: **The tiger eats meat.**

All elephants have thick, wrinkly skins.

★ So we can say: **The elephant has thick, wrinkly skin.**

You will find this kind of sentence in your wild-life books.

Write what each of these sentences means.

1. The owl hunts at night.

   This means that **all** owls . . .

2. The swallow migrates in winter. This means . . .

3. The cow eats grass. This means . . .

4. The ostrich cannot fly.

   This means that **no** . . .

5. The tortoise cannot climb trees. This means . . .

★ What did you notice about the last two?

How are they different from the rest?

Fascinating fact

The tortoise is a very long-lived animal.
One giant tortoise, called Samir, was supposed to be 269 years old.

48